PRE-OBITUARY OF ROBERT HENRY MAYES FROM BELLVILLE, TEXAS

BY ROBERT MAYES

To : Bellair
Thank you for sharing!
This is my story.
Love your courage
R Mayes RPh (Retired)

Pre-obituary of Robert Henry Mayes from Bellville Texas
Published by Cotillion Publishing

ISBN: 979-8-218-16533-8

Personal Memoir

Printed in the United States of America.

PRE-OBITUARY OF ROBERT HENRY MAYES FROM BELLVILLE, TEXAS

CHAPTER ONE

1953 was a memorable and important year! The U.S. President was Dwight D. Eisenhower, the first color television sets went on sale, *Peter Pan* premiered, deluxe toy sewing machines were marketed, and a bouncing baby boy was born to Lois and Bracey Mayes in Bellville, Texas. Not important to most, as what film was released, the newest toy gadget, or who was in the White House, but to these parents, nothing was more important than that baby boy, especially to my daddy. You see, I was the second born, and back then the common thought was that a man needed a son to carry on his name. This sort of thinking I seemed to adopt until much later in life.

My sister, Cynthia, and I grew to love country life. Mostly I remember sunny days where we spent our time looking at the clouds to find shapes that looked like animals, cars, trees, or whatever. There weren't many toys, but we had fun with jump rope, hopscotch, and baseball with a ball and a stick. My mother played with us for the most part, but many times the two of them had things to do inside. I would then take an old tire and roll it up and down the dirt road, running, laughing, and making sounds like the muffler of an old car. During the summers while Daddy went off to work, Mama got extra cash picking cotton for local farmers. Cynthia and I would play outside until dark or until we got hungry. We were lucky to have a garden, chickens for eggs, and a Jersey cow for milk. When food was scarce, we made sugar syrup and sopped it up with bread. One of our favorite treats was clabber milk with hot corn bread. Sprinkle on a little sugar and 'man ole man!'

Life was so simple then. Everyone had a role to play. Whenever you were out of line, the first indication was the way you were summoned. "Robert Henry, get your behind in here!" I don't recall ever wetting my pants but those were scary times. They simply used the methods of those times to raise us. We lived about a hundred yards behind our church where my uncle (Mama's brother, Red) was the pastor. We were taught religious values as best it could be, although I strayed from time to time. Those times, however, were not so simple for my parents. My dad told me later why we weren't allowed to go inside town with him to get groceries. (We lived outside the city limits in the 'country' as it was referred to back then). He described it as embarrassing and demeaning (although he used other words) as he had to relinquish the sidewalk if approached by a white man on that same side. Another brother of my mother, John (Uncle Dee), showed me a tree not far from our house where a black man was hanged. They endured much. I was probably about the age of thirteen before they were allowed to vote. It was a different time, although violence is still all around us. That little church, Mount Zion Missionary Baptist Church, continued to emphasize, 'Keeping your hands in God's hand' and 'Love thy neighbor as thyself.'

Being raised in this environment, I wasn't very good at self-expression. I remember when my mother passed away, my mother's sister (Aunt Bee), asked Cynthia, "Is Robert okay? He didn't say very much." There were times as I look back that I should have voiced my opinions or feelings, but didn't. Life's curves can push you out of your comfort zone. Recognizing this and seeking to prepare myself, I sort out a speaking club called Toastmasters. While not being able to express my feelings for the passing of my mother to my family, I was able to do it at a Toastmaster's club meeting before people who didn't really know me. From that beginning, many speeches were done at a club meeting before delivery to other audiences. The first speech that I want to share with you is the one that I was asked to do by my daughter, Julie, at her wedding. It's entitled 'Curves of Life'… Enjoy

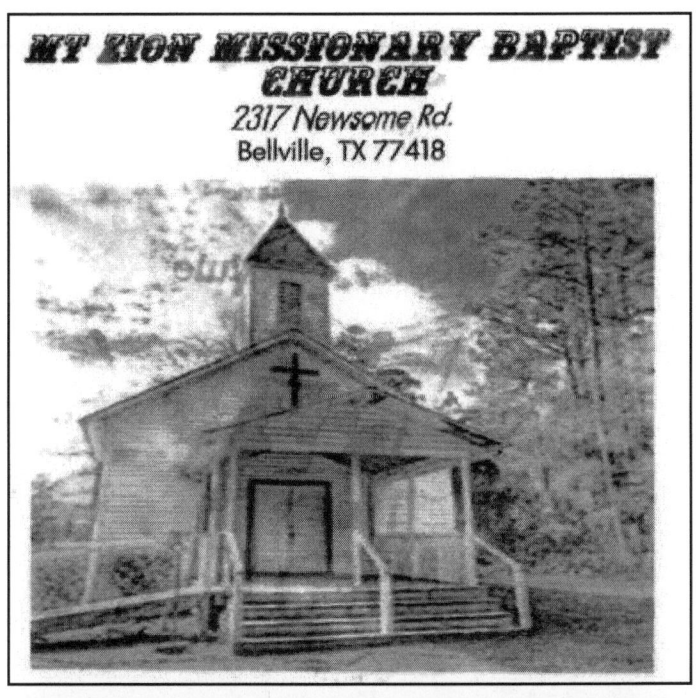

CURVES OF LIFE

"If there be trouble, let it be in my day; so that my Child will have Peace."

- Thomas Payne.

Good Evening, Fellow Toastmasters I'm so glad to see so many here tonight to hear this icebreaker speech which is designed to let club members know more about the speaker. I can be more personal. I remember back in high school, girls seemed to be planning farther ahead. I thought of that recently when a young college girl that I worked with, answered my question; "Are you and your boyfriend thinking of marriage?" She replied, "He doesn't know it yet, (and in a loud /forceful voice) **BUT THAT'S THE PLAN!"** (pause). Fellows, I gotta say, they mature much earlier and we're lucky if we ever catch up. Do you remember as a teenager, thinking of your future; the college you might attend, your job or profession, your marriage, or did you even want kids? I remember at Bellville High my sister Cynthia wanted two kids (a boy and a girl). The girl was to be named Sabrina. I think the boy's name was waiting to see who would be the husband. She actually got two girls who had two boys each and oh my, do they keep her busy! We just say, life threw her a curve. As for me, I played football, basketball, and was on the track and field team. I wanted a boy. Well, I got a girl and what a curve that was. She was full of frolic and a joy to be around. At the time, I had just purchased a home, I was driving a Porsche, and my credit cards were near the max, and yet the milk and diapers had to come. My sister called my mother and said, "Robert has gone crazy. He bought cloth diapers and hangs them on a line in the backyard" From here, the years started swiftly rolling by. I don't recall if her first words were 'Mom or Dad' but a word that she used a lot was "Um hummy." She did have an appetite (and I'd learn later, for life). As she grew there were always questions: "Where are we going today?... What are we gonna do?"... What, when, why?! Oh my goodness! I figured out early that a girl needs to know answers early. I then would get up early and with my list I would tell her, "We are going here today...", "We are doing this thing..." and have the whole layout of our day before her. And oh yeah, as a man I would sometimes miss and would get the look, the little hand (on what would later be her hip), and those piercing words, "Well, I thought you said…"

I remember thinking that those were the good years, especially after one particular incident. There was a house party at a classmates' home and I was to take her. As I watched her walk downstairs with a top that was cut too low and a skirt that was hemmed too high, and before my brain could say "What the what?" my mouth said, "You'd better get back upstairs and change! I know you're not wearing that outfit!" I thought that we would argue for forty-five minutes and I wouldn't have to take her. But NO, she changed and we went. I was to pick her up at a certain time but I decided to arrive early. I cruise by the house (and with a double take), I see my daughter outside under a tree with some boy, in that same inappropriate outfit! I was livid!

Things like that, well, you could probably figure that it's gonna happen. But other things, not so sure of. I gave her books that inspired me, like *Think and Grow Rich* by Napoleon Hill. Did she read it? Unsure. We'd talk about money, even before Dave Ramsey, with lessons from Kevin Trudeau. Will she manage money well? Unsure, the jury is still out. Every Sunday after church, it was Chili's and we called it Baby Back Rib Day. While the music played, I would quiz her on the artist and the name of the tune. When she moved to Houston, she called me with so much excitement. "There's this singer that makes the kind of music you like!" I get to the concert at the Houston Livestock Show and Rodeo and it's Chris Stapleton! I raise her on Motown and she loves country! Who'da thunk it?! **When** I didn't get that boy, I just thought that God had a sense of humor. But more than that, because for that curve, I realized HE knew what I needed. I look at life differently now; it's not about me, anymore. I matured. I'm more patient, tolerant, flexible, observant, and yes indeed, wiser. Yes, simply because of the way she was or more correctly, the way she is. Thank you, Julie.

CHAPTER TWO

As I begin my journey in 1953, so did many things that I love even today, although many in memory. This was the year that we got the first recording of Elvis Presley. If you didn't love the King, you were (presumed to be) a 'different bird.' Just, FYI, my daughter, Julie, shares with him the same date of birth. My sister, Cynthia, would get so excited as we watched our black and white Westinghouse television set, to see Elvis perform on the *Ed Sullivan Show*. WOW! You just had to be there! It was during this decade that my mother added three members to our family. My stepfather, Floyd whom I would 'color this man father, I think I'll color this man love' (A line from a song that came much later). I got two more sisters, Linda and Brenda. We grew together, shared good and bad times, and our love for each other grew naturally. I loved to laugh! *The Red Skelton Show* began in '53 and kept my attention. I even had my own comedy routine later while in the cotton fields. I would pretend to be a Southern Baptist preacher, making my family and cousins laugh and take their minds off the dreadfully hot work that lie ahead. I supposed that I laughed too much because no little girl would take me seriously. In elementary school, I was smitten with a little girl named Patricia. I thought that she was the prettiest thing ever. When she came around, however, I'd get tongue tied. I kept laughing and being silly until my first real girlfriend in high school. This was Bobbie. Being so afraid of losing her, I became the most possessive person ever. I'm still conscience of that time, even today, that I work to give a person room to grow but also claiming my own space. One day she did the unthinkable and gave me the boot, deservingly so. I stopped laughing. Then came the college years, where I became more focused. I met so many beautiful people. I went to a baseball game with Marty. Our racial difference seemed to cause her some stress. Certainly, I understood that. The lady that got most of my attention was Juanita. I felt that I wanted to belong to something/someone. After some time, sadly, we separated as well. I felt destined to be alone. I hung out with Jesse, who was living his gay lifestyle. When I would visit, he'd whip up the best meals. His cakes and pies were to die for! You could not, however, ask for one of his recipes because you'd risk getting a real good cussing. Oh well, he had his religion and I had mine. I tried spending time with my cousin, Will, and his new wife. My father told me, "That's not good… your cousin is married now!" Throughout the many relationships (or opportunities), it wasn't until I joined Toastmasters that I had a chance to reflect while putting words together for a speech. This was not a sad speech as I have found more love than I could ever share on paper. I wrote about this in a speech for my club in 2007 and called it 'Shades of Love.' Enjoy.

FALL 2007
SHADES OF LOVE

Greetings Toastmasters and guests, I regret missing the last meeting where the toastmaster Mary Jane came with her theme on Country Music. Although I probably knew many of the songs and artists, there is a particular section of music (as defined by someone many years ago) called Silly Love Songs. This may encompass country, pop, or other forms (but maybe not hip-hop). The words of one song stuck with me over the years and I want to share them with you. The lyrics go like this: 'From the beginning to end, 365 days of the year, I want the same old love, Baby. And all I want to do is keep on loving you, the same old love…' Not very many words yet powerful stuff by Anita Baker. I want to share with you tonight, love that's dear to all of us (close and personal), love that we hear about in the media (distant or dark, even spurious if you will) and finally want to share a bit of history on language, to connect my thoughts. I get a call from my daughter (then 19), "Hi Dad… going to the mall… Need $80… love ya bye!" I told her that she's breaking my heart. If you can't say, I love you and good bye, just ask for the money and go. My sister heard this and laughed, then said "I love you, Robert, I need $100." Even on my job, "I love you, Robert, what's for lunch?" I heard that just today, and yes, I bought everyone lunch (pizza). Hearing 'I love you' was dear to me and yes. I would pay for it. As for love of the spurious type, it was the year 2000, a report was released that said, in America we house two million inmates. Many of you are world traveled so I ask, what do you think? Is it mental disease, the need for money, or the need for love (or belonging)? No time tonight to go into all the crimes but I want to share one incident. Recently in the Garland/Richardson Texas area gang activity was on the rise. We were told at a community meeting that in the initiation process, one must knock on someone's door, when it opens, shoot the person in the face.

Because of our need to belong or need for love? We're reduced ourselves to being simply animals, it seems. Members must feel a need for love or a need to belong that's so strong, it evolves in a very distant and ugly way. I recently heard a lecture on the evolution of languages. This wasn't biblically connected but a scientific research project. The word for rock (or stone) on the coast of Africa could be connected to a word on the island nearby or around the world according to migration and time. Even though the record of transitional sequences is quite incomplete, the evidence taken together clearly supports the thesis that the different linguistic kinds we now observe, grew through gradual transformations from earlier ancestral forms. So what are we saying? If you consider that although we are different, we came from the same or similar source, (just like the rock) which should make our understanding of each other and our loving of each other, easier!

I have a dream, that one day, we lay down the bearers that separate us. I want to say, "I love you" to a different culture without feeling that I've crossed a forbidden line because of our obvious differences. I want to say "I love you" to the same gender without feeling awkward or being ridiculed. Do you remember when a young boy, energetic and cheerful, was called happy and gay? Can you hear the whispers now? 'I knew it!... Come out, Queen... Get out of that closet.' Hard to live down. I want to say "I love you" to a couple, without feeling that I've plunged a wedge in the sanctity of marriage. I have a dream today. It may not happen today or next week, but planting this seed today, it may grow with one or two of you and spread (migrate) throughout common thought. In that day, from beginning to end, 365 days of the year, we all can get the same old love.

Madame Toastmaster

CHAPTER THREE

The reputation of our president, Dwight D. Eisenhower (from Denison, Texas) varied over his years in office (1953-1961) and afterwards. He was remembered early on for his frequent golfing and fishing trips. There was some talk that he left most of the business of government to White House assistants. His vague and sometimes incomplete answers to questions at press conferences led many to wonder if he had a handle on the issues or even any idea as to how to solve them. However unfortunate, during the '50's, President Eisenhower was labeled the 'Do Nothing' president! Years later, historians would rate him higher compared to other presidents for several reasons. He did not lead the country into war, and six months after taking office, negotiated an armistice in the Korean war. He made decisions that stimulated the economy such as supporting the construction of the Interstate Highway System. He resisted panicked public demand for huge increases in military spending. He was tight on spending while maintaining a strong economy throughout his term. Also doing these times there were actions taken to achieve civil rights. President Eisenhower did not try to change contemporary thinking about race issues by speaking out in favor of the Civil Rights Movement. He was in favor of action to end racial segregation, but was unwilling to use his moral authority as President to advance the movement. He remained a gradualist who believed that changes in individuals' hearts and minds, more than the passage of laws, would eliminate racial barriers. Just going through this period of time seems like ancient history. Actually, it wasn't that far back. Recent numbers show that during that time ninety nine percent of registered voters were white, with many obstacles facing the black voter. America was narrow-minded as proven by the next President, John F. Kennedy, who was Catholic. Tons of anti-Catholicism sentiment surfaced in America. It appeared that anyone running for this office had to fit a cookie cutter profile. Anyone or anything different would get great push-back. It would take thirty-eight years for the hearts and minds of Americans to soften enough to approve a 'black candidate.' Could it be that there was too much confusion as to what we should call ourselves? Once done, we could rally behind a common denominator. For sure, it took some time to get through the various designations: colored, negro, Afro-American, non-white (not Mexican), black, and some others that weren't so pleasant. Religion and race have always been huge issues while no one has ever considered heritage. This came to me as I explored Ancestry.com. As I scrolled down the pages many were labeled 'negro,' while just as many were labeled 'mulatto.' Curiosity pushed me to find the meaning, which is one having a parent that's white and the other parent that's black. Clearly, we are more connected and interconnected than a quick surface view could reveal. Not having a social platform to ask the many questions that I had, I decided to take this to my Toastmaster club in a speech. I thought that this would be something we would all discuss and laugh about it later, but to my surprise it seemed to stir up negative emotions. Obviously, a difficult topic at that time. This speech was given in 2017, entitled 'Questions ,Questions, Questions'… Enjoy.

FALL, 2017
QUESTIONS, QUESTIONS, QUESTIONS!

A young lady lived with her father and her five-year-old son. On a particular Friday night in September, she prepared her son Aamni for his bath. Mom says, "Come Dear, let's get our bath." Aamni replied, "Why?" and Mom said, "Because you are dirty." He asked, "Is there school tomorrow?" She said, "No." By now she starts to remove his clothes. "No school… so why?" with a rise of reluctance in his little voice. Losing some patience, "Come on, Honey, and stop with the questions." She turns for a moment to reach for something and away he went. Naked little Aamni scampers to the living room where his

PawPaw is reclining. Laughing and screaming loudly, "PawPaw, PawPaw, save me!" PawPaw sits forward and says, "Son, do you believe with all your heart that Jesus is the Son of God?" With both hands raised, Aamni replied, "Yes!" PawPaw smiles and embraces his grandson. Questions may cause frustrations, yet the correct answer could save you.

G.E. Fellow Toastmasters I've often heard that there are no bad questions, except the ones not asked! Today, there are so many questions: Should we tear down all historic statues? Should America recommit to Afghanistan and send 4,000 more troops? Why are we so divided on the race issue in this time in history? This last question prompted me to ask, how do or should we define Black? In a presentation by Williams (Smokey) Robinson, he states that, "if you have one drop of black blood, then you are Black!" I suppose that if this were common knowledge we would not have questioned the presidential campaign of then-Senator Barack Obama.

First a little background. On June 11, 1776, the Articles for Confederation, (the original constitution of the U.S.) was proposed and agreed upon, November 5, 1777. However, Maryland refused to sign until New York ceded their western lands. After ratification, Maryland joined. John Hanson signed the articles and was voted by congress to be the first president of the United States. A moor (depicted by Europeans as being black) who established The Great Seal of the U.S., where every subsequent president has used to sign official documents. He set the fourth Thursday of November as Thanksgiving (still today). The variable that wasn't initially thought through: a moor in the heart of enslavement period as president? The Articles was replaced by the U.S. Constitution in 1789 with a new president, George Washington.

With that, comes another question: Were there other black presidents? Thomas Jefferson (1801-1809) had numerous children with Sally Hemings (his mulatto slave). It was said that his mother was a half-bred Indian squaw and his father was mulatto from Virginia.

Andrew Jackson (1829-1837) had a step-brother that was sold into slavery. Jackson's mother was a white woman from Ireland and his father was a black man.

Abraham Lincoln (1861-1865), whose mother was from an Ethiopian tribe and his father was African American.

Warren Harding (1921-1923) wouldn't deny his 'Negro' heritage. Calvin Coolidge (1923-1929) proudly admitted his blackness. His mother's maiden name was Moor.

Dwight D. Eisenhower (1953-1961) had a well-known anti-war advocate mother. Ida Elizabeth Stover Eisenhower was half-black.

Unsure if anyone ever questioned these men. If so, President Obama would not have been labeled as the first. And maybe people of color would have felt more inclusive if known, thus less racial strife in the streets? I'm not sure, it's just a question.

CHAPTER FOUR

The decade of the '50's was good to us; we survived, and then came the '60's. My mother was busy again, adding three more members to our family. We were blessed with my brother, Floyd, and two more sisters, Dovie and Kathy. My parents embraced us all with love and care. I remember thinking at that time, how much more crying was done by my sister, Dovie! If, however, you get an opportunity to hear her sing, then you would appreciate the fact that she developed those vocal cords very early in life. Together, we all attended Union Center Elementary. Mrs. Crezetta Jackson taught the first and second grades. Mrs. Clara King taught the third and fourth grade classes. Mrs. Clara Newsome taught the fifth grade only. Mrs. Idell Canty taught the sixth and seventh grades. The eighth grade was taught by our principal, Mrs. Elthena Teel. She once said that other schools looked down on her, saying "the nerve of her, a female, showing up as the coach of the basketball team!" These teachers not only taught more than one grade (or class), they had to stand in as coaches, advisors, psychologist, mentors, nurses, and yes, disciplinarians. If I only had the opportunity to tell them how great they were, I would scream it loud and clear for all to hear! I know now the importance of teaching during those early years. If I wasn't serious and got caught playing too much, Mrs. King with a growl in her voice would say, "Alright Little Mayes, I'm gonna come over there and tan your britches!" This however could have happened at any grade, one through seven. It was the eighth grade that I went to O'Bryant Elementary (the white school). This would be the first of many experiences where I was the only person of color. I now, jokingly say, "the only spot in the house." Looking back, I was rambunctious; however, all of us siblings were obedient and listened to our parents. There was a lady that lived with her mother, a couple of miles down the road from us. When her mother became ill, my mother felt that they could use some help around the house. I was volunteered, and well, I couldn't resist. Mrs. Coats was beautiful with long, white, hair although some days there was a blue tint to it. She was loved and appreciated in the neighborhood, and oh, so talkative. I was glad to listen. She once said that my mother and kids her age "had it good" beause they were able to go to school. To think of her words later in life, I realized that if my mother were able to go to school and my grandfather wasn't, slavery was not that far back! All of a sudden it wasn't ancient history anymore. I am closer to that period than I care to be. I began to understand why things were different for us. The difference in education led to different word usages, pronunciations, and sounds. Mrs. Coats' first name was Lily. We pronounced it 'LieLee.' The 'i' had the 'i' sound. One of my cousins lived on a street called Lisa Mae Lane. We pronounced it 'LieZa Mae.' The name Tom sounded different at O'Bryant Elementary. We were accustomed to hearing the 'o' sound. The letter 'r' had a different sound as well. When I hear that vernacular while visiting older friends it warms my heart, it brings me back home, it excites me and somehow it saddens me. After attending different colleges and universities and meeting so many beautiful and interesting people, the importance of increasing one's vocabulary became apparent. The attractive aspects of Toastmaster weren't just speaking or listening but learning new words. This was the duty of the grammarian. One of my speeches highlighted this duty. It is entitled 'JUST SAY THE WORD.' Let me share it with you now. Enjoy.

SUMMER, 2020
JUST SAY THE WORD

You may write me down in history with your bitter twisted lies, you may trod me in the very dirt but still like dust I rise. You can shoot me with your words, you can cut me with your lies, you can kill me with your hatefulness, but just like life, I rise. – Maya Angelou

Good evening, Fellow Toastmasters,

Once weekly, we meet to better our ability to speak and just as much to listen. One duty, however, that's more important than I initially realized is that of the grammarian. Oh, so important, increasing our vocabulary is key! There may be words that are totally new to us, some perhaps not used as much and still some that we frequently use. When given an opportunity to speak we must use it, just say the word, or risk a small financial charge. I want to share three words, although used at different frequencies, to make my point or better to yield a larger message. These are parallax (PARALLAX), differential, and problematic.

Parallax is the effect whereby the position or direction of an object appears to differ when viewed from different positions. (*repeat*). A simple example of this: while driving on the highway… when you look out the window, the electric poles seem to zoom pass, while a tree one hundred yards away appears to slowly drift by. In order to humanize this point, I will look at education, specifically that of the Historic Black Colleges and Universities (HBCUs). In 1862, the federal government's Morrill Act, provided for 'land grant colleges' in each state. Under this act, some institutions in the North and West were open to black students. However, seventeen (17) states, mostly in the South could NOT see this happening. Thus required their Institutions to be segregated and generally excluded black students. Congress had to pass a second act, the Agricultural College Act of 1890, requiring states to establish a separate college for black students. In Houston, Texas, the powers that be, built a college next to the University of Houston in 1927 (Houston Colored Junior College) and renamed in 1934 (Houston College for Negroes), again renamed in 1947 (Texas State University for Negroes), and finally the lasting name in 1951 (Texas Southern University), my Alma Mater. U of H saw me differently.

The next word is differential, a technical term used more in politics or mathematics. Means differing or varying according to circumstances or relevant factors. Examples (keeping with humanizing): the suffrage movement spot lighted the differential achievements of boys and girls. Or, the differential achievements of different races peaked prior to integrations. Staying with the plight of HBCUs, one of the first was Fisk University (originally Fisk Freed Colored School). Founded in 1866, in Nashville Tennessee, would take students from age 7-70. Enrollment jumped after several months from 200 to

900. This indicated the freedmen's strong desire for education. From 1915 to 1925, the President of Fisk, Fayette Avery McKenzie, developed this to be the premier of all black universities in the U.S. in spite his differential view of his student body. He coaxed the biology professor to spy on the students. Quite frequently, their mail was opened and reviewed before delivery. A female student was accused of stealing and although no proof, she was expelled. If students complained, they were expelled. He was called unjust and unreasonable: could not socialize, a boy could not walk a girl to class, and definitely no holding hands. He summed up methods with the rationale, 'they are too sexual!'

Problematic is defined as constituting or presenting a problem or difficulty. For America, problematic was to teach or not to teach. For black leaders, problematic was WHAT to teach.

Booker T. Washington, educator/reformer urged blacks to accept discrimination for the time being and concentrate on hard work and material prosperity. In one speech, he said, "Education whether of a black man or a white man, gives one physical courage to stand in front of a cannon and fails to give him moral courage to stand up in defense of right and justice is a failure!" Yet he seems to suggest that HBCUs only teach agriculture and mechanics.

On the other hand, a graduate of Fisk University and the first black Harvard graduate, W.E.B Du Bois, maintained that education and civil rights were the only way to achieve equality. Less would mean that blacks were second class citizens. Political action and agitation were the only way to achieve this. He broke from the ideas of Washington, wanted HBCUs to teach agriculture, but medicine, law, political science, Et cetera, Et cetera.

Our toastmaster journey must increase our vocabulary and we look to our grammarian for that! Knowing and using different words allows us to paint different pictures. It is clear that education is the key to prosperity of a nation as well as the individuals within. Week after week, just say the word and use it when you leave. Knowing more, changes the parallax, diminishes differential and solves so much that's problematic.

Hopefully using the plight of HBCUs through these three words, not only enlightens but leads us to a place of less hatefulness and bitter twisted lies: when we learn together, we all shall rise.

CHAPTER FIVE

It wasn't light outside as I lay still in a shared bed. I could hear Mama in the kitchen making lunch for Daddy. He worked for the Texas State Highway Department. He always left early for any jobs he had. He would say, "any man caught sleeping when the sun rises, is just plain trifling." I remember seeing him, as we drove by, aboard this huge tractor while pulling a large mower. The sides of the roads of Austin County were very well kept because of my daddy. Before that, he did everything from farming, ranching, with side jobs like breaking horses, which even today, I think was pretty cool. Shortly after leaving, my mother called for us to get up. We were going to the fields to pick cotton for Mr. Quehauer. Later in the summer, we would do the same for Uncle Dee along with his sons Wesley, Charles, and William Douglas (W.D.). It was a challenge competing with them. Charles would always pick the most. I only wanted to get one hundred pounds of cotton. This was an important marker as we were paid $2.00 per hundred pounds. Many times, I didn't make it. By the time school rolled around in September, I was able to buy a few clothes. I enjoyed prancing around my new 'kicks,' which I liked to call my new shoes. As kids this was our first introduction to work. Chores were things that we just had to do and not considered work. Those fields left memories of long hours on hot days.

We had one car with no air conditioning. By most standards we were poor folk, however, we didn't know it. We had a couple of horses, a few head of cattle (with a Jersey or Holstein for milk), a flock of chickens, hogs with numerous squealing pigs, and sometimes we had a family of little white rabbits. No need to call ourselves poor, because we had everything. I even had a long stick that I tied a string onto and would go up the road to a small tank for a little fishing. Later in the year when cotton production dwindled, hauling hay for the local farmers was my next big job. I got to say, the heat and the dust had a profound negative effect on me. Later, while choosing a profession but not knowing exactly what I wanted, I simply wanted an inside job. I did not care what it was. I was done with cotton, hay bales, fixing fences, pulling and hauling watermelons, or anything else that had anything to do with outside labor.

Looking back, my parents were very strong people. They raised seven children and taught us basic life skills: hard work, spiritual guidance, honesty, integrity, and the importance of helping one another and others. Being raised in this environment shaped the way I would approach things throughout my life. I do regret times where I didn't speak up or didn't move on an idea or project, mostly because of self-doubt or fear. My involvement in Toastmasters enabled me to speak on my growth in this area. The speech is entitled 'Wear It Well.' Enjoy.

WEAR IT WELL

An old man said to me, "Boy, what you doing?" "Just killing time," I replied. "Darn you," then a pause, "Time is such a precious commodity, don't kill it!"

Good Evening Fellow Toastmasters;
Coming up in a small Texas town in the '60's, I never, early on, considered the elements of success. Through time and experience, I believe that there are three things that should be considered: what you wear (on your back), what you wear in your mind (thoughts), and what you wear in your heart (feelings). Let me explain.

I didn't think that I was poor. I remember sitting next to a boy in school who cut up a card board box, inserted pieces in his shoes to cover the holes in the soles. Well, as for me, I had two pair, school shoes and Sunday shoes. We had what we had! Dressing for success wasn't even a thought.

Later (and older), through different schools, an idea was frequently passed around: 'Thoughts are things. Be careful what you think about." I wasn't this profound thinker. In fact, most of the things on my mind came directly from a black and white television. I saw a man burn the American flag. Should I enlist in the army or defect, as seen on TV. There were racial conflicts all around. I was deeply moved as I saw my shows (kid shows, cartoons), begin to use profanity! That was a lot for my little mind, and I hadn't started dating yet! *pause*

Things I wore in my heart were inherent of the times. My house like most of the homes around us, the man ruled. If we kids got out of line, we got a good beaten! Only heard 'bout spankings much later in life. After much to drink on Saturday nights, it was Mama's time. From these and other events I had unfounded doubts, fears, suspicions, and confusions. Confused, I was, for thinking there was a club who spent time toasting and drinking! Okay, maybe not. But I joined Toastmasters anyway. First, I noticed that the toastmaster of the evening was dressed for success. They ran the meetings and looked like leaders. Each member who competed in contests dressed for success, like they were going to win. (Hoping it would work for me today).

This was a mind-altering experience for sure. When I would get up and they looked back at me (with various looks). I was glad they couldn't see the footprints on my tongue, because I stepped on it more times than a few.

But each time they were oh so encouraging with a caring and loving manner, that I begin to think more positively about me, my success, and that of others. This phenomenon takes place week after week after week.

It changed my heart from the doubt, fear, suspicions, and confusions, to the knowledge that I could encourage others, lift them up, and touch them in a positive way simply by wearing a caring, loving heart. Time IS a precious commodity. So while you have time, be thoughtful of what you wear (on your back, in your mind, and in your heart). And for your own success, make darn sure, you wear it well!

Spring 2020

21

CHAPTER SIX

The nights were truly black during the '60's. There were no streetlights in the Stephenson community outside of Bellville. Early mornings we could the rooster crowing, just as the sun came up. Mostly foggy days beginning with dew covering the grass. As Cynthia, Brenda, Linda, and I rushed to get ready for school, Mama made grits for breakfast. She made her own bread back then and I never forgot the smell of her fresh bread. She'd let it rise overnight before baking. As time changed, she would buy Sunbeam light bread. It came in a plastic bag with a picture of a white girl with yellow or orange hair. It wasn't as good, but it was convenient. Many folk struggled as poverty flourished, so the government begin to subsidize food for the poor. We had to show up at a designated place inside Bellville on a particular day and time to get our allotment. I distantly remember the block of cheese, the powdered milk, and the canned goods which included processed meat. We called this 'commodity day.' I could see that many in line needed it much more than us. I went to my mother and told her that we didn't need it. Soon we stopped attending commodity day. I stressed that we had all that we needed, however, we did not have luxuries but I didn't know that. On the way into town, there was a public swimming pool. A sign was posted saying 'Whites Only.' I was fine with that because no one I knew could swim or even wanted to. The local restaurants hung similar signs on the front door and the door to the back said 'colored.' As the powers that he, wrestled with the idea of integration, our school Union Center was closed and we were all shipped to Cochran, the then white school. Then all the students that were there moved to O'Bryant Elementary, inside the city limits of Bellville. This was funny. The white school was now a black school. The following year, my mother asked if I wanted to attend O'Bryant and I really didn't think about it and said 'okay.' I had heard that a friend of mine was going, so I wasn't worried. Once getting there I didn't see Robert L. As a joke, we all called him Leaky because he would laugh so hard that tears freely ran down his cheeks. I learned later that Leaky was placed in the Special Ed class. I only saw him at recess. He had met a friend named Donald Ray. As for me, there were no other blacks in my class. I met some incredibly bright and friendly students. There were others like Patsy who ran up to me and screamed, "Damn Nigger, Damn Nigger!" It took me a moment because I didn't understand what she was saying. Then, oh… I got it. On occasion, there would be a boy who acted like he wanted to fight, but I don't recall having to. I realize now that this was only a microcosm of everything going on in America at that time. There were sit-ins at restaurants, riots on college campuses, civil rights marches with just much racial tension throughout the land. It was my name as next to speak at my Toastmaster club. I addressed this subject and entitled it 'Time on Race.'

TIME ON RACE

Greetings Fellow Toastmasters,

Throughout our history the human race has focused on many difficult issues, some more than others. I want to point out some things that we're studied deeply and others that deeply needs our attention. This formula: $F1 = G \, m1 \times m2/ \, r2$, was created in the 1700's by Isaac Newton. It's called the law of universal gravitation, which states that any two bodies in the universe attract each other with a force that is directly proportional to the square of the distance between them. WOW, only a great mind could come up with such. If I had to formulate a hypothesis from this formula, it would be this; any two people (doesn't matter their weight) that are in a long-distance relationship are bound to fail! Silly of me… I know, no way to prove or disprove. A twenty-four-year-old, lay in bed watching a fly on the ceiling. In his mind he drew a grid that contained lines of latitude and of longitude. From this he could always tell where that fly was located, until it flew. This added another dimension, the final step, which is time. This led Albert Einstein to his Theory of Relativity. This gave way to the idea that time isn't the same everywhere due to gravity. This was proven correct with a clock in the valley and one on a mountain top, by Steven Hawkins. Cool stuff… Something else, however, that is more practical is finding the relationship between space, control, and user component by Dr. Gladys West (a black female) who discovered the Global Positioning System or GPS. WOW! Although much time has been spent on atomic physics, nuclear physics, and quantum mechanics, there are numerous other things that beg for our time Examples are global warming (which concerns so many), oceanography (as most of the earth is covered with water and we know so little) and maybe race relations. Let me share a couple of events to see that this could make our nation better and stronger. A boy was born into slavery and he was called Denmark. He was purchased by a sailor named Vesey. Once grown, he won a lottery and bought his freedom. His desire to know and teach the bible led to many meetings involving the church. Because he was so popular, he was accused of planning a revolt. For this, he was tried and hanged. After review, 150 years later, it was found that the mayor planned all of this for political gain. The city of Charleston, S.C., is now building a monument to honor his name, Denmark Vesey.

George Bernard Shaw said, 'We are made wise not by the recollection of our past but by the responsibility of our future.' Clearly, it's not only that we maybe should spend time on race issues but it's our responsibility! One more story, please. After 1865, the end of the Civil War and after civil right battles of the 1960's, and after the first president of color, not much has changed. Of the sixteen states that have a city called Cleveland, let's focus on Cleveland, MS., who's facing a lawsuit. They have two middle schools, one on each side of the railroad track (one of them white and one of them black). They have two high schools, one on each side of the railroad track (one of them white and one of them black). On Monday, May 16th, 2016, a Federal Court ordered desegregation plans, 60 years after the Brown versus the Board of Education which said, 'Separate but equal has no place in public schools.' Hopefully noting that we have done much but issues like race begs for our attention. On our club level as our membership is dwindling and we lost the likes of Shirley, Jeanie, Cynthia, Gilbert and others, the time on race is now. We can then see the larger picture which is a human rights issue which makes each member, each club, this country and the human race better and stronger.

Spring 2016

CHAPTER SEVEN

To grow up in a small town is special. To leave and return, whether for school, work-related travel, or even a vacation, there is a comforting feel that we all get. Personally, I think the air smells better also. True especially for us who grew up in Bellville, Texas. This unique place began when Thomas and brother James Bell, who immigrated from Florida in 1922 and settled in the area of present-day Bellville in 1838. The brothers donated 145 acres of land for a townsite in 1848, the same year (platted and by popular vote) was called Bellville. From its origin, the town was to be centered around the courthouse. Although young I remember seeing this magnificent structure during the few times that my sister and I rode into town. We were in our first car which was a black Chevrolet Powerglide. Peered out the window in awe at what would be called the most remembered courthouse in Texas. It met with a tragic fire in 1960 but was rebuilt in the same place while throughout, continued to entertain court cases. This brought some debate to my opinion that this was a beautiful, friendly town with beautiful, friendly people. Here many criminal cases were settled. Let me share a couple of the more notable, which occurred in Austin County prior to the courthouse. A man named Alois Peters who lived in Austin County, feared that someone wanted to harm him. On a particular night in 1895, he chose to sleep differently by placing his head where his feet were normally. A perpetrator with a shotgun filled with scrap iron, aimed at his head and fired, hitting his feet. The bone was shattered to such a degree, the blood lose was too much that during surgery he died. The man with the rifle, Clem Strauther, was caught and tried. On the other end of the county, a widow Dora Emshoft had just brought in her cotton crop and money. She was with her nine-year-old daughter, Cara. At the time of the robbery, Clem was shot beneath her right eye. Clara recognized Andrew 'Buck' Chappell and identified him before judge Teichmueller during trial. Both men were sentenced to hang at the same time, March 18, 1896.

The landscape was different when I lived in Bellville. There were no other ethnic groups, like Asians, Mexicans, Native American Indians. Although a photo of my maternal grandmother showed clearly her American Indian blood. The reason I didn't mention other groups is that our communities were fairly close-knit. It was referred to as us and them. Also, there weren't as many news media streams. Every so often a petty thief and an occasional fight at the joint we called James Place.

Most of the time, this was directly related to excess drinking, but a few times someone said the wrong thing to someone's wife or girlfriend. There weren't any drugs to speak of, although later it would wreak havoc on our town, especially the black towns folk. As time passed and the town grew so did crime particularly violent crime. We would hear of rapes, stabbings, shootings, and yes, murders. There was a case of two school janitors who sighted the body of a sixteen-year-old white girl, nude except for her sweat socks. She was a member of the Bellville High girls' volleyball team visiting Conroe High for a scrimmage. The police viewed those who found the body as prime suspects. The interviewing officer said, "One of you two is going to hang for this! Well, since you're the Nigger, you're elected!" Sad, but that's the way it was, us and them. I had a chance to address violence in a speech. It was entitled 'Violent Triggers.'

VIOLENT TRIGGERS

Daily, we awake to news: Two were shot and killed in South Dallas; A domestic violence suspect arrested after hours-long standoff; North Texas Hospital report spikes in severe child abuse cases.

GE. **Fellow Toastmasters**, many like Tom, Roger, and others (myself included) were raised during a times that the language on Television was tapered.

Seldom did we hear of a person being killed (never serial killings) and for sure no kid brought a gun to school.

How, then, can we ignore this trend of increased violence? A recent article said that this past century as compared to previous ones, suggests that violence is in decline and we are safer now than ever before. I noted later that this reported on homicides but did not include domestic, child abuse, gang, hate crimes (racial or sex orientation related), in schools, prisons, or in sports. I will probably summon more questions than answers, but I want to look at violence seen in government/politics, in religion, and in times of a crisis. Since recorded history, violence and politics have been intimately related. Of all the empires looked at (Sparta, Egypt, Russia, etc.) I chose the Roman Empire. There was extreme violence in the Roman Society which is said, may have contributed to their downfall. Violence against individuals was considered an offense against the community. Such people were hunted down, taken through a court system where they typically were given the death sentence: carried out by throwing them to the beasts, burning alive, or crucifixions. All classes and levels in society were subject to violence, which mirrors our own society?... April 14, 1865, while attending the Ford Theater to watch a play called 'Our American Cousin,' President Lincoln was shot. September 5th, 1975, Lynette 'Squeaky' Fromme attempted to kill President Gerald Ford. Seventeen days later her roommate (both from the Manson Family Cult) Sara Jane Moore tried again but failed. March 30,1981, John Hinckley Jr. attempted to kill President Ronald Reagan. There were some rumors that Vice President Bush, who was well acquainted with fellow Texan and Oil associate, John Hinckley Sr. was seeking to fast tract to the presidency. Reminds me of the Roman dictator who was stabbed 23 times, Julius Cesar. **Religious Violence** is a term where religion is either the subject or the object of violent behavior. Many factors incite violent behavior and religious attachment or loyalty is just one. Violence is inherent to human nature and as humans we are easily swayed by emotions and irrational behaviors. Some examples of religious violence, past and present:

The French Wars of Religion, Protestant-Catholic Conflict in Ireland. 911 and other terrorist attacks, the burning and booming of black churches.

Solutions??? Well, there were many suggestions for example, people need to focus on the positive aspects of their religion and cultivate tolerance. Difficult, if not impossible, especially in times of a Crisis… which looms with extreme uncertainty and extreme fear. During these times, (I.e. Rona or Corona virus), we hear stories of nurses standing against protestors and getting spit on from those who simply need to get to work. Reports of Dr. Tony Faucci giving incorrect treatment methods with numerous doctors suggesting alternatives (the correct approach). This type of propaganda is leading us toward hatred. Important to note here that this crisis has caused an increase (60-80%) of watching television. So… more violence through the screens of the computer and cinema? How is this effecting our youth?

One of the most needed, least known skills in our world today, is Conflict Resolution! We don't learn it in school, at home, in the media, or in the streets. So… we act on impulse, leading to misunderstanding and violence. Dr. Dudley Weeks, an international conflict resolution facilitator, says: People in conflict should look beneath their difference to discover their shared needs. Building on the foundation of shared needs people can then become partners, creating new solutions together. The key: Stop reacting with anger and fear and look for common ground, for beneath the differences that divide us, there is so much more we have in common, this beautiful planet we call home. Join me in an effort to decrease violence! It begins with each one of us.

CHAPTER EIGHT

It was the fall of the 1967-68 school year that I attended O'Bryant Elementary. I was to take my first step toward manhood by defying my mother. After being told that I could not play football, I was pressured as my friends talked in excitement about staying after school to join the football team. I didn't have a car and if I couldn't find a ride home, I'd have to call my mother. It would be a long wait in front of Lange's Grocery Store near the Enco Service station. I pondered a bit then ran to the fieldhouse. Getting fitted with the uniform, pads, shoes, and a helmet was exciting. Practice was a new experience. I wasn't too keen on getting hit by some huge lineman but I felt that I could out run most of them. This was the second year of integration which meant that we (black, colored, negro, or some other name) kids could now attend Bellville High in the nineth grade (next year for me). Before this, black students were bussed to the nearby town of Sealy for their high school education. Although there were some tense moments during class and recess, we came together for the good of our football team. Coach Vick was firm yet positive. We were all treated equally and to this day the friends I made are still friends like Ernie, David, Ricky, Warren, and others. By the way, my mother, although furious for a few moments, finally accepted the idea that I was going to play football. I won't mention the sad faces, with much begging and pleading, that helped my case. The next year starting high school there were no black coaches and certainly no black quarterbacks. The first of the black coaches was Coach Sears. Soon I got the opportunity to play quarterback. It was only for a short while, but I was told in later years that I was the first quarterback of color at BHS. The times gave me fond memories although there were arguments and fights. It was always a big deal when Leroy, Dennis, or Ronnie was involved. Although we thought that our condition was bad, our experiences seem to dwarf that of the blacks who lived one hundred years before us. Let me share one story that took place in 1868 during the early years of Reconstruction. After the Georgia Constitution of 1868, thirty-three Black men, all republicans (known as the Original 33) were elected to the Georgia State Assembly. These were some of the first black legislators in the country. After the election, the white Democratic majority conspired to expel or remove all blacks and mixed race (mulatto) members from the Assembly. It took place on September 3rd, 1868. Representative Philip Joiner, one of the expelled members, made plans to march and rally a course of 25 miles to the courthouse square in Mitchell County to protest the expulsion. In each passing town, more people joined until there were almost 300 men, both black and white. They carried guns and weapons as it was customary and legal at that time. Things were seemingly going well until they reached the town of Camilla and was met by Sheriff Mumford Poore and a citizens committee. The sheriff wanted them to surrender their weapons or there would be violence. Joiner and the marchers refused and continued. Poore immediately deputized the local whites who gathered. As the marchers entered the square they were fired upon from all directions. Fifteen were killed and forty were wounded as the remainder retreated to the swamps outside the town. Over the next few weeks, white men from Camilla went throughout the countryside, beating and warning blacks that they would be killed if they voted in the next election. Joiner survived the attack and later gave testimony to the Freedman's Bureau. This intimidation greatly reduced the republican vote, thus none of the Original 33 returned to the Georgia Assembly. In 1976, the Black Caucus of the Georgia Assembly honored the Original 33 with a statue that depicts the rise of the black politicians, on the grounds of the Georgia State Capitol in Atlanta.

Over the years, I have come to learn that politics affects all areas of our lives. It became obvious that the best way to win in any area of life is by building relationships. In my club, I attempt to convey this message in a speech I called 'Bridges.' Enjoy.

BRIDGES

There are illustrated essays on bridge structures from prehistoric to present day, by Judith Dupre, a New York Times bestselling author. It's a fascinating journey from stone, brick, then iron, and finally, steel. When asked how did all this come about, the answer, simply by necessity. Good evening, Fellow Toastmasters. The word bridge is defined as a structure carrying a road, path, railroad or canal across a river, ravine, road, railroad, or other obstacle. Although a firm definition, the word bridge can be used in other ways, that is socially, politically, and personally. My history consists of a short time as a band member. In doing so, I realized that a song does not consist of a list of verses. They are connected by a bridge. It made sense now to hear James Brown saying, 'To the bridge y'all, to the bridge…' The song by Paul Simon and Art Garfunkel, 'Bridge Over Troubled Water' is about providing comfort for someone in need. A bridge from bad to better times, if you will. This whole idea of music as a bridge can be found on musicbridges.com, which is dedicated to the creation and development of international collaborative music projects and related special events to serve as a cultural link between nations and foster greater understanding among the worldwide human community. In politics, there has to be numerous bridges that connects the various opinions, ideas, and beliefs of this melting pot of cultures in which we live. As Speaker of the House of Delegates for our state association, the Texas Pharmacy Association, I had to familiarize myself with Robert's Rules of Order. Here, a type of motion called an Incidental Motion, is used to suspend the rules. Although you can't interrupt the speaker, it does require a second, with no debate necessary, yet it requires a 2/3 vote to: set aside rules that interfere with the desired action. Finally, bridges can be used in a personal way. A writer once said, 'bridges are metaphors for everything in life.' As I was about to enter the stage while in San Antonio Texas at an association conference, the then-president called me by another name. The Dallas delegate was angered by this. She said, 'You've been active too long! You're served on committees, held officer roles and they can't get your name right! That's not right!' The simplest bridge could have connected this seemingly huge gap in understanding. "I apologize" or "forgive me" would have worked fine as we are all subject to a mistake. Other bridge words are, 'please, thank you, are you okay, and can I help.' This reminds me of Stephen Covey's words, "first seek to understand…." **Bridges** can connect great divides like land divided by water, or nations of different cultures, or everyday personal events. I beseech you here and now in this club to consider bridging our differences in order to become a stronger club.

OUTSTANDING CLUB OFFICERS
January – June 2014

OUTSTANDING PRESIDENT
Robert Mayes, ACS, CL
Trinity Toastmasters

Our club is one of the oldest in District 50, and only once, in 1986, has our club reached President's Distinguished status. In fact, the last time our club was even Distinguished was 2004. When our new club president took the reins in 2013, he presented our club executive committee with written goals, and a plan to get us to President's Distinguished.

We scoffed, said that would never happen. Then he set out to prove us wrong. He invited friends, relatives, spoke at the men's group at his church, urging all of them to attend and join. He printed flyers and took them to the businesses near our meeting place to advertise our club. He called past members and urged them to return to our club.

He didn't stop with new members. He earned his CL and ACS awards within a month of each other, setting an example for others. One member, who had put off finishing his ACS for at least 10 years, did so due to our president's leadership. His efforts brought us 5 new members and a new banner from the district. As an encouragement to the new members giving ice breakers, he hired a photographer, to tape their first speech who will return for their 10th.

As the end of the year approached, two more members earned CC's. Even then, he continued urging us to bring more members. By then we were all caught up in the excitement of actually achieving the PDC award. When we did, we all knew it was because of the leadership of our president, who worked hard and believed. I believe Robert Mayes deserves to be honored as the Outstanding Club President for 2013-2014.

OTHER NOMINEES
Tyler Evening Toastmasters – Adrian Dunklin
Twin Cities Toastmasters – Allan Wren
TNT/Town North Trendsetters – Charlene Sims
Pepsico Presenters – Cindy Vogel
Stonebridge Toastmasters Club – Eric Bowie
Premier Presenters – Gary Applegate
Verbal Expressions – Nancy Bateman

CHAPTER NINE

My hometown, 'The Bell of the Bluebonnet State' was special then, and yes, even to this day. I had the opportunity to attend class with many amazing people, athletes, and scholars. I want to mention a few: Neal, Wayne, Joey, John, Curtis, and David, along with Cindy, Verbaline, Vonnie, Shirley, Marlene, Verbean, Janet, and many others whom I share fond memories. My high school years were filled with highlights. The short list is this: showing a blue ribbon (Brangus) heifer in the county fair, receiving an award through the AG Coop program at the FFA (Future Farmers of America) banquet and taking a photo with my mom, attending our school prom in both my junior and senior years, dancing the cotton-eyed joe at the annual Spring Wing Ding, co-hosting the annual talent show with Eddie, was chosen to be a member of the student council and the national honor society, rejected an offer to play football at Eastern New Mexico State University as I could not tear myself from my love at that time, and finally, believe it or not, I was elected to be Mr. BHS runner up in my senior year. Throughout all the experiences, the bulk of my time was spent on athletics. Although when asked, I could not recall a golf team or a tennis team. It was football or basketball then track and field which overshadowed baseball, golf, and tennis. Track season was an individual sport where I participated in sprint and distance races, relays, hurdles, as well as the high jump. Although it appeared that I moved freely about socially, looking back, I mostly stayed in my lane. Ronnie and I noticed (and made a joke) that while the student body assembled in the gym, if one stood on center court and looked toward the stands, going right to left, the crowd slowly gets darker and darker. Funny then but true, we generally congregated among ourselves. Even after a huge football game where BHS wins, the meet up place was 'The Hill' owned by my Uncle Alfred, where we got snacks and a drink (coke), played pool, and danced to the latest from the jukebox. Whether win or lose, The Hill would only be filled with folk that looked the same. I once heard that the most segregated time of the week is Sunday morning during our perspective worship hour. I'd like to add a close second to be Friday night after our high school football games. There was an event that we had an opportunity to close the gap. During the annual Spring Wing Ding, the student body elects a King and Queen for these festivities. It was during our junior year that my friend, Robert, whom we all called Pete, won the honor to be King. The female elected to escort him did not attend. The idea of two different races marching together was unthinkable. In fact, there were only two races back then and sometime later there were Mexican, Asian, Indian, African, and others to come and live. The commonality of all is the contribution of their women. I felt lucky as I had five strong sisters, Aunts (Bee, Jessie, Ruby, and Sadie) who constantly instructed me, powerful church ladies (Ms. Lilee, Elnora, Cousin Georgia) and incredible teachers (Ms. Jackson, Mrs. King, Mrs. Newsome, Ms. Canty, and Mrs. Teel). After meeting and interacting with other races I began to realize how important women are to the world. My mother for me, stands supreme. I suppose that they had to be strong as there was much to endure. A date that sticks with me is July 13, 1853, because of the 13th day of the month and 100 years before I was born. When I moved and settled in Dallas, Texas, I found out that on that date in Dallas, the first black female was executed for killing a white male whom she was loaned to. You might say that was a black mark or a serious negative aspect of Dallas, but no, it was just America. I became involved in numerous ventures here and realized that I needed to improve my public speaking skills. In comes Toastmasters International (TM), a great club, but I wanted to do a quick lookback, historically. During a time of black and white televisions, when moms were expected to stay home and raise the kids, Helen Blanchard, who worked at the US Navy Research and Development Center and oversaw 130 government employees, sought to improve her speaking skills. She called TM in 1970 and was told, "Sorry, no females allowed!" A call two weeks later from TM, saying they have changed their minds. On the application, the gender column was overlooked as the local chapter used the 'H' in her first name to stand for Homer. Three years later, Toastmasters International began accepting women. In the year 2007, I prepared a speech that gave my views on women, their struggles and strength.

A DOMINANT FORCE

Help me please, to complete this sentence: Behind every good man is _____!

Good Evening, Fellow Toastmasters

I remember getting punished (a whipping, back then) as a boy and hearing my mother's voice, "Boy, if you don't stop that sniffling, I'm gonna give you something to cry for!" Mean or powerful? When my daughter was about five, she said, "If my boyfriend talks to another girl, I'm gonna kick his butt!" My mouth dropped. They are a force from the time they begin to speak until, until, oh I don't know, maybe Alzheimer's disease. A force behind the rise of every good men. Throughout history women have gone through a lot with regards to their duties, their rights and freedoms, and their hair and clothes. From the birth of this country (new world) women, which consisted of Native Americans, European Caucasians, and African Slaves, lived with similar responsibilities. These were childbearing, childrearing, and food preparation. Although important, still they were second class. From the day the pilgrims arrived, the idea that women were inferior, ruled. In the beginning (of the Bible) it's noted that the woman came from the rib of the man with a nature of being easily persuaded, thus man was kicked out of the garden. Paul's writings in the New Testament tells of their limited roles in the church. Probably because women were easily influenced, and for heaven's sake, prone to gossip. Pilgrims and our Founding Fathers came with the idea or equal belief of 'manifest destiny' which allows them to take land, freely kill, and beat his wife (to the point of death). Out and out killing her was frowned upon. This idea led to 200 years of 'Suffrage.' Starting in the 1700's efforts to uplift women begin. They had no voice in politics, their workplaces, or decisions in their marriage. Their actions were called civil disobedience, beginning with propaganda. An example was a campaign slogan which said, 'Women were better at housekeeping, so they should be allowed to be involved in the housekeeping of politics.' In their workplaces, conditions were awful. Enclosed in dirty work areas and many times locked in, preventing them to leave. These were called 'sweat shops,' with no real wages and no rights. In New York, 1911, there was a great fire. With no fire escapes, it caused 150 women to perish. Their movement led to an eight-hour day, minimum wage, and voting rights (August 18th, 1920. The 19th Amendment).

In the home, it would take more time. If a wife said 'no' to sex, it could lead to punishment. In 1870, Victoria Woodhall, testified before a Congressional committee on sexual hypocrisy within the marriage relationship. Family matters are more difficult to legislate. It was more than twenty years later, in 1893, that the lawful beating of the wife was repealed.

On a lighter note, styles and fashions have changed. I had a night job and worked the counter as a lady approached to make a purchase. I asked, "So, when are you due?" She replied in a very ugly tone, "I'm not pregnant!" It was the clothes, just hanging loosely, so I couldn't tell. Long ago, the corset was used to tighten or train the midsection to a desired shape. Later, the girdle was used, but now, nothing! Before the 1900's, the more robust women were attractive. The long-time granny panties has been replaced with the thong. So, what's next, nothing? Back then breasts were not an issue as most women breastfed the young. The ankles attracted sex. If a dress was cut high enough to see the ankles, the woman would be labeled a slut, tramp. The plight of the woman is a story that parallels that of most ethnic groups. A story of trials and tribulations and yet many victories.

Note: I had a bottle of Noni Juice and shot glasses for the men.

Good Men, please stand with me and lift your glasses. I would like to make a toast: 'To the women here tonight and any who has influenced your lives, LADIES, WE SALUTE YOU!'

CHAPTER TEN

The influences on kids today are so numerous. With the television, computers, internet, and a host of socially connecting sites, I am glad that I came from a more genteel time. I remember being bored as there wasn't much to do. Yes, there were chores: slopping hogs, feeding and milking cows, but there was time to ride our horse, Chester. We did not socialize much, yet we were occasionally allowed to visit school friends, none of which lived close. I was probably a teenager when we got our first color television. From there the images that influenced me were sports figures, politicians, and entertainers. However, the first two could be subsets of the third. During high school, although competing I felt small but we were all the same, being at a UIL Class 1A school versus the prestigious 4A it is today. Without a lot of fancy equipment, a self-made high jumping rack propelled me to compete not only at BHS but Blinn Junior College (as a walk-on to their track team), as well as high jumping with an intermural squad at the University of Houston. There was, however, a tight end, Ted Koy, who went on to play after BHS and made the town folk proud. Any other influences for me came from watching that television set like Earl, The Pearl, Monroe who played college basketball at Winston-Salem State University. I tried hard to imitate his style of play which was so exciting. You can catch an old school video of him playing professionally with the New York Nicks. As for baseball, I did not really like, but watching Reggie Jackson was a treat as every time he was up to bat, we just expected a homerun. Another figure played a bad guy in our favorite movies after his football career. That was a smooth transition for Jim Brown because he was the baddest guy on his team.

There were politicians that were endearing. Our Texas Senator, Barbara Jordan, was a source of great pride. I liked her history as she came from a close-knit family, went to Texas Southern University, and many times was the first person of color, or the only one, at different events. This mirrored my own personal story. Another person that I would see on the campus of TSU was Mickey Leland, a congressman from the 18th district in Texas and chair of the Congressional Black Caucus. I was able to walk up to him, as I recall, and invite him to a banquet at the college of pharmacy during my term as Senior Class President. We were all shocked to hear of the airplane crash that took this fellow pharmacist. Houston, Texas housed numerous prominent leaders. I remember being amazed, impressed, and excited after hearing a young speaker named Sylvester Turner, who later moved up the political ladder.

The entertainers that graced the stage and screen were true to their game. The music was played by the artists, versus using computers. If you were a dancer, you had to be good to keep an audience. The quick feet of James Brown had all of us fellows trying hard to be like him. From the screen, the comedian Flip Wilson gave us many memorable lines like, "What you see is what you get!", or "The devil made me do it", and "Don't order one for the road, 'cause the road is already laid out." From the show *All in The Family*, Archie Bunker called it like he saw it. "I ain't no bigot. I'm the first guy to say, It ain't your fault that youse are colored." Also, "Anybody that goes to see a psychiatrist ought to have his head examined!" Looking back, I'm unsure if political correctness helped or hurt us all. It was the early 70's and I needed to decide on a career. I was too small for sports, not connected enough for politics, and did not possess entertaining skills like singing, dancing, or acting. Just a quick recap: out of high school, I attended Blinn Jr. College in Brenham, Texas. From there my application to the University of Texas (Austin) School of Nursing was rejected, stating 'we have too many applicants. Please apply next semester.' My high school friend, Warren, suggested that we both apply to pharmacy school. We were accepted at the University of Houston. From this point I spent time in and out of school for various reasons and held numerous jobs during those times. I was a truck driver (liquor), brick layer (apprentice), painter (contractor), auto mechanic, and various others. I didn't have much ambition. After hauling hay, fixing fences, tending to cows and hogs, I simply wanted an inside job. I didn't know then that you can have anything you want, and I tell all the young people that I have a chance to interact with, "Just Dream Big!" With the influence of Dr. Louis Williams and two classmates, Carolyn and Nena, I strived to be a professional. I worked with the voice of my mother's brother, Uncle Red (Alonzo), in my head, "If you can just help somebody along the way, your living will not be in vain." Most of all, however, I wanted to make my parents proud. After going through the embarrassing ordeal of scholastic probation and scholastic suspension, I applied to Texas Southern University's College of Pharmacy and thankfully was accepted. Later on as a toastmaster, I was asked to give a humorous speech which is difficult to write. This is my attempt to do it as I recall experiences as a pharmacist.

WHITE COATS

Good evening, Fellow Toastmasters

Numerous professionals go to work wearing white coats: dentists, nurse practitioners, doctors, barbers, and pharmacists, to name a few. Do you remember your first dental appointment? Many of you, like many that I know, had such a bad experience that they did not want to go back. I hear many times of the doctor's appointment that spiked someone's blood pressure. White coats just seem to trigger FEAR. On a particular occasion, I went to a different barber. Upon entering the shop, although my hair was long, it was fairly even all around, or at least shaped such that it was socially fitting. Upon leaving, one side of my head was clearly cut lower but he couldn't see it. I learned later that my initial comment to him sort of rubbed him the wrong way. I said, "I smell something awful..." I didn't know that was his breath! Lesson learned: be careful what you say to those wearing white coats, especially if they are about to serve you. Recently, I was in line to pick up my prescription at my local drug store. As I waited, the conversation ahead of me went like this: "My doctor said that he okayed my prescription so why isn't it ready?" The petite pharmacist addressed this fairly large, formidable adversary, "That is correct, sir, however, your insurance says that it is too soon to fill." He slaps the counter and growls under his breath, "Lady, if I don't get my medicine and I die, it's all your fault!" A sweet little gray-haired lady, looked to be about eighty or so, said softly, "If he was to die, this world would be a much nicer place." My eyes got as big as a baseball because I didn't know what was going to happen next. To my surprise, he simply snarled at her and walked out. We appear to show fear for professionals with white coats but not for the ones behind the pharmacy counter, even when we show up with all sorts of folderol. It's not like getting a haircut which grows back if not just right. It's getting chemicals, foreign to our body, to be ingested, injected, or inserted. That alone should trigger FEAR! Let me give you a few examples. The prescription drug Crestor, whose generic name is Rosuvastatin, is used to lower cholesterol. When filled and delivered to patient, there is a sheet or literature with it designed to help navigate toward less fear or more understanding to maximize health and safety. At first glance, you got to be a chemist yourself! It says, 'Before using, tell your doctor if you have an allergy to rosuvastatin or any part of this drug"! Do you know the chemical structure or any part (head, tail, or any area in between)? There is a section on Cautions: If you are 65 or older, use this drug with care as there may be more side effects. The very next sentence says, it may cause harm to the unborn baby. To put it here I felt the manufacturer was truly concerned about seniors and their sex life. In Possible Side Effects, we know first of all, that any chemical could led to an allergic reaction: rash, hives, with peeling skin that's red, swollen, or blistered (with or without fever). Besides these, this drug may cause a very bad muscle problems with pain, tenderness, or weakness, which may lead to kidney problems. It is mentioned, however, deaths rarely happen. One could try an over-the-counter vitamin like niacin, which is used for niacin deficiency, but in higher doses it can lower cholesterol. Niacin, like any other drug, could cause an allergic reaction. An additional issue with niacin is signs of high blood sugar like confusion, feeling sleepy, more hunger and thirst, fast breathing, or breath that smells like fruit. WOW! It just occurred to me that I could have told that barber that niacin helps the body make sex and stress related hormones, which it does. Most men want to know this whether needed or not, where fruit breath is a plus. There is a drug called Tikosyn (generic name of dofetilide) which is used to treat certain types of abnormal heart beats. Like most drugs again, there may be allergic responses. Long before you get to the side effects there is a warning: there is a risk that this drug may cause another type of abnormal heartbeat which may be deadly! Oh my goodness! I suppose that if I had to choose an abnormal heartbeat, I would keep my God-given one! Besides, this latter one could see chest pain or pressure, dizziness, or passing out. The silver lining here is that at the bottom of the page we have, https://www.fda.gov/medwatch and the FDA number 1-800-FDA-1088. Is this not scary?! Oh well, help is only a phone call away. Just one more example, Xifaxan (Rifaximin), which is used to treat loose stools (diarrhea). The very next line says, used to prevent brain problems! Really?! I had the urge to slip a couple in my pocket (for me and a few people I know). The list of possible side effects starts the same with signs seen in an allergic reaction. Then it says, this medicine can cause diarrhea even though it's given to treat diarrhea. If this occurs, do not treat loose stools without checking with your doctor. WHAT!!?? Heaven forbid it's 5:01 P.M. on Friday. Near the bottom, after headache, dizziness, belly pain, feeling tired or weak, it reads: These are not all of the side effects that can occur. So, if you encounter a white coat especially at the pharmacy, be kind. It's to your advantage. You meet great people and they are there for You to live Happy and Healthy.

CHAPTER ELEVEN

It was the early 80's and I was finished with school. Now it was time for advancement as well as reflection. I suppose that parents of the new students of pharmacy were much higher achievers than ours. To go back and visit the campus I noticed that students were driving much finer cars, I mean, BMW fine! This was mind-blowing knowing that I left the university and moved to Dallas on the back of a Harley Davidson Sportster. That first winter was a chiller. In fact, it snowed heavily as I dealt with new surroundings, new job, no friends, and new elements of the weather. I walked into a small car dealership at Hawn Freeway and Elam Road. A cheerful, upbeat salesman asked, "What kind of vehicle are you looking for?" I replied, "I don't care if only has three wheels, as long as it has a heater." I ended up buying a light blue Oldsmobile Cutlass Supreme because it reminded me of blue skies and warmer days that I left behind. I was pleased with this small accomplishment, but I didn't fare so well with the locals. I found it difficult to warm up to folk. Unlike Houston, when I'd meet a Brother while walking out and about, we gave a chin up to acknowledge one another. In Dallas and the same or similar scenario, our eyes didn't meet. The guy would look down or away. Although troubling, I resolved in that I was here to carve out a living, not to fix the ways of the people. I expressly found employment with a retail chain pharmacy organization called Revco. For whatever reason, I sometimes walked from my Oak Hollow apartment. After some time and meeting guys in the complex, I ventured out to socialize with a couple of them. We ended up in an apartment in another part of town. Someone pulled out a Bunsen burner, a spoon, and a tourniquet. The hottest thing at the time was a combination called 'T's and Blues.' Up to this point I had only read about this in school. Although naive, I thought to myself, 'What if the cops kicked down the door? My career would be over.' "Do you want some?" I replied "No", in a convincing tone as to not show my nervousness. I made it out safely and decided to find entertainment alone for a while. I liked the theater, remembering those days in Houston. I chose to see a play at the Majestic Theater featuring Carol Channing. If there were any in the audience that looked like me, well, they were working. It took me two years to get over my missing Houston, as that city seemed to be moving forward. Once I was in Dallas, Houston elected a female major, Kathy Whitmire, and a black police chief, Lee Brown. I was impressed. Now it was time to advance my professional career. I did not move into management right away and years went by before I got the opportunity. I could see, however, the advantages in joining the pharmacy association. Locally it was the Dallas County Pharmaceutical Society, which was under the umbrella of the statewide Texas Pharmacy Association (TPA). Initially the association was dominated by independent pharmacists. These were pharmacists that owed their own pharmacies which I attempted, although unsuccessfully, some years later. It took a long time before the chain pharmacists would come on board. Many of these pharmacists worked at Eckerd Drug, and for a while there was a huge Eckerd section at the local meetings. From this group came many exceptional pharmacists like Carrie, Stan, Bob, Chris, and numerous others who did much to advance the profession. We were given a great deal of direction from a compliant officer named Cy Welch. Carrie held leadership positions and was highlighted in several TV commercials. Stan was a respected Area Manager with Eckerds. Chris campaigned and was chosen to serve on the Texas State Board of Pharmacy. Before then, he served as the president of the Dallas Chapter of TPA, renamed by this time to the Dallas Area Pharmacy Association (DAPA). During one of his speeches, I was inspired to become more active in our association. The following year, I ran for president and was given the opportunity. We had a good year as my objective was to increase membership. In doing so I invited, although not all at once, a minister for the invocation and prayer, a masseuse, a poet who recited his original work, several comedians, an artist that shared his paintings, and occasionally a live band, to name a few. With a little entertainment and a lot of liquor, I suppose that one could say that our meetings were quite lively. So much so that I was asked to do it again. A couple of years later, it was Chris who campaigned for me to serve as TPA's Chair of the House of Delegates during the annual convention. I had to study a bit to get comfortable with Robert's Rules for Order, which began with a course through my Toastmasters club. Although I felt that my performance was okay, I was asked to do it again and again and again. When returning to my club after the convention, it was my time to speak. It was easy to find material as I mostly chose things that were occurring in my life. From this experience my next speech was entitled 'Orderly Manner.' Enjoy.

ORDERLY MANNER

Good evening, Fellow Toastmasters.

It was a general in the United States Army shortly after the Civil War (about 1876) that after attending many fraternal, community, and church meetings, he became concerned by the absence of consistency in conducting such meetings. General Henry M. Robert compiled a manual to help these groups run their meetings in an orderly manner. Today it's known as Robert's Rules of Order. This week as our club prepared for our membership campaign, having a chairperson was invaluable. Not just for putting up flyers or posters, but negotiating and handling motions, like main motions, privilege motions, or subsidiary (most uses to amend) notions. Without a chair, emotions can really stagnate any meeting. You need also a quorum or a specific number of people to transact business. For sure, not all discussions require Robert's Rules, but would aid smaller discussions and certainly needed for larger meetings. Tom, a fellow toastmaster, and loving husband, was in trouble. He had forgotten his wedding anniversary and his wife was really ticked off at this. She told him, "Tomorrow morning, I expect to find a gift in the driveway that goes from zero to two hundred in under six seconds! And it had better be there!" The next morning, Tom was up and out early. When his wife awoke several hours later, she looked out of the window and noticed a small gift-wrapped box sitting in the middle of the driveway. Confused, she put on her robe, ran to the driveway, and took the box inside. Once opened she found a brand-new bathroom scale...! Tom is not yet well enough to have visitors. In this case, other rules may apply (*pause*). A family of four is planning a big vacation trip in the coming week but there is a dilemma. Mom and Dad aren't home yet and the nineteen-year-old son leaves his job early to find his fourteen-year-old sister there with an unknown boy in the house. He calls Mom. She comes promptly, and the discussion begins. Mom begins in a demanding tone, "You WILL tell your father!" (A sort of main motion.) In her efforts to save herself, she suggests putting it off, indefinitely. (Postponing indefinitely is a move to kill the motion.) Her brother wants to amend, adding, "Beat her first, then tell Dad!" Mom wants to postpone 'till after the vacation. "This is really going to hurt your father." The daughter wants to limit the debate. However, to suspend the rules requires a two-thirds vote, but there is no quorum. The son wants to extend the debate (a privileged motion which because of great importance gets precedence). Mom wants to call for the Previous Question (a motion to close the debate) because she is too upset. Finally, the main motion is laid on the table (a subsidiary motion that sets aside a pending motion), hopefully until after the vacation. These rules are good in any meeting setting, but there should be a chairperson that is not emotionally attached. Also, a quorum is important. Without both of these, order cannot be maintained. I would like to look at current events and give another example. Listen with your imagination. There is a meeting on the other side of the clouds. At the head of the table (although called many names) is The Giver of Life. Surrounded by many angels, the meeting gets underway. The motions begin: "As it is time, I move that we bring Ed home!" The motion is seconded and the debate begins. "He has done enough!" says one. "There is more to do!" says another, and on and on they debate. Then stands The Grim Reaper, "I want to amend the motion and add two more names, one of Charlie's Angels and the man in the mirror. The crowd gasps as this is seconded and the debate begins. Which angel, someone asks. What man, asks another. The Grim Reaper stands again, I move that we amend the amended motion to delete Charlie's Angel and the man in the mirror and add Farrah and Michael. Seconded. Someone in the back shouts, "I move that we amend the secondary amended motion to choose another angel." Mr. Chairman says, "I can only entertain a primary and secondary motion to amend. Your motion to choose another angel is out of order." As the debate rocks on, the Grim Reaper reminds the crowd that it has been our tradition to bring home three at a time. Someone begins to list the qualifications of Ed and begins to tell why this is not right. The chair reminds the maker of the fact that any debate must relate to the motion at hand, and that is to amend. Thus, "you are out of order." As time is growing short, the chair asks, "Are you ready for the question, on the motion to amend to 'bring home Ed, Farrah, and Michael?'" This is properly seconded. "All in favor, say Aye… and all oppose say Nay." After listening, the Ayes have it and the main motion is amended. Now the main motion is repeated (we bring home Ed, Farrah, and Michael), properly seconded, no more discussion, and the vote is taken. The ayes have it. A chariot will be sent forth. Amendments are the most used motions and makes getting through business smooth and orderly. This is out of order but I want to share a story that was out of order, unusual manner, yet smooth. Little Billy was sitting on a park bench munching on one candy bar after another. After the sixth one a man on the bench across from him said, "Son, you know that eating all that candy isn't good for you. It will give you acne, rotten your teeth, and make you fat." Little Billy frowned and thought for a moment, then replied, "My Grandfather lived to be 107 years old." "Oh?", replied the man. "Did your grandfather eat six candy bars at a time?" "No!" said Little Billy, "He minded his own business!"

CHAPTER 12

The nineties were like any other decade as I was determined to have as many experiences as I could, realizing that time is swiftly passing by. You might think that I lived through the words of an old blues tune by Louis Jordan, which I first heard performed by Ray Charles which said this:

"Hey everybody, let's have some fun
You only live but once, and when
You're dead you're done
So let the good times roll"

Great advice but suggests that I was a huge party animal, NOT! Coming from a small town and having certain values, this couldn't be farther from true. Now good, clean fun was okay, but I lacked the nerves to go all out! A very attractive and sexy co-worker asked if I would go with her and her friend to the 'killin' flo' (a bit of Houston vernacular at the time). She was surprised and disappointed when I refused. Although sleeping with two females at once seems to be a fantasy of many men, well, I just didn't have the balls.

Anyone that visited and passed through my kitchen could see a note posted to my refrigerator which read: 'I don't want to be a kept citizen, humbled and dulled by having everyone else look after me. I want to take the calculated risks, to dream, to build, to succeed or fail, whichever way it goes. With God's help, I want to live it to the fullest.' I just wanted to do it my way.

Although the tone of the nineties was set by MTV and the theme of *Friends*, I missed much of it as a workaholic, family man, and a seeker of adventure. Working as a pharmacist was rewarding. It's always best to do the best you can at any job. Back then, pharmacists did everything needed to service our patients. Compounding wasn't yet specialized so we made what preparations that had to be. On one occasion a young lady brought a preparation back. I remembered preparing her initial prescription. "It didn't look right from that other guy!"

She trusted me which gave me a good feeling. I made sure the pills were grinded finely which gave the preparation a smooth consistency, with a neat and easy to read label, covered with tape to preserve the appearance.

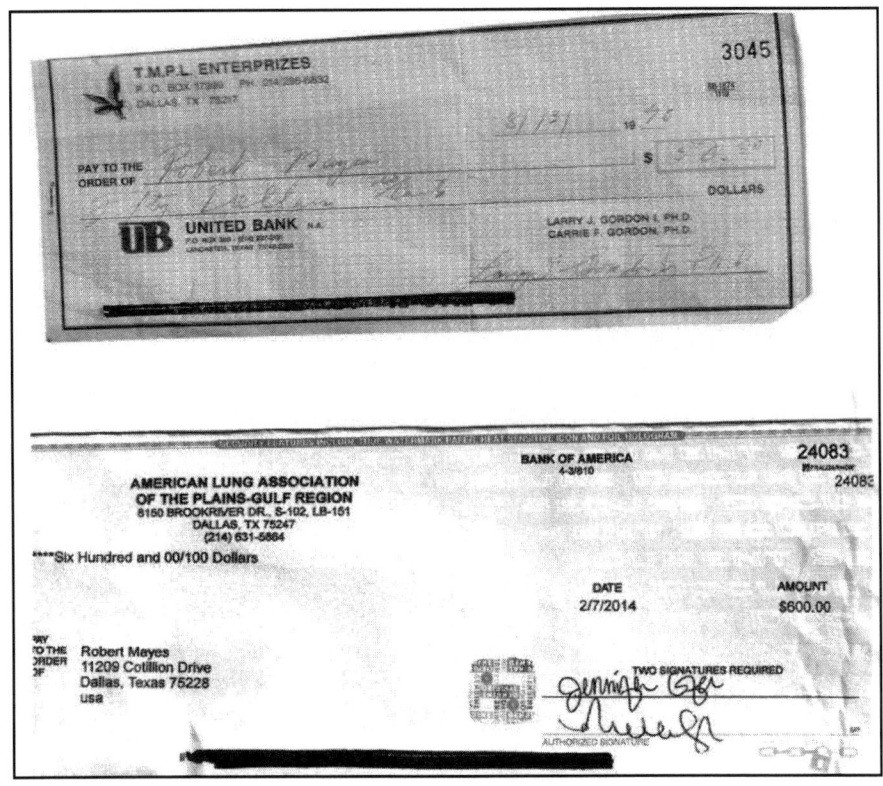

Not only was it satisfying with patients but working as a relief pharmacist for many of the Eckerd Drug stores in and around the Dallas metroplex, it was great to hear pharmacists ask that I return to help in the future. I was told, "all I had to do was to come in and start filling prescriptions when I work behind you." They appreciated not having to come to work and start their day by filing reports, or prescriptions, taking out trash, or just tidying up. I didn't take much time off because I enjoyed spending money on Mama and Daddy. Although Daddy wasn't too happy when I gave Mama a mink coat, a mint stole, and a diamond ring. I understood later. Helping my family was a big deal. I did shift my focus when my daughter was born. Those early years were nervous ones. We changed babysitters numerous times. They all did something or another that made us look for someone better. We never found that person. My sister, Kathy, became upset with me and called my mother, "Robert won't let me keep that baby!" To say that I was a bit protective, well, you'd be correct! I didn't read the Baby Book, but took ques from other parents. My Japanese friend said, "we put our kids in everything that we can and let them decide what they like and want to pursue." That was the beginning of lessons in dance (tap, ballet, jazz), swimming, piano, drums (bongos included), karate, acting, modeling, and anything else offered at school. I had the pleasure of coaching her middle school's basketball team. It was there that I realized that she was not a runner, but her swimming skills were outstanding. With her it was one adventure after another although many adventures followed. One adventure, after acquiring an insurance license, I sort a career in sales with a company called A.L. Williams (now Primerica). It is very important to dig in and learn as much as possible, regardless of the discipline. I was stunned to learn of the history of insurance sales. Whole Life policies, which were more costly, were sold to black families. The agent would knock on doors every month to collect premiums. The families were not aware that these policies were quietly called 'Nigger Insurance.' They simply were not privy to the fact that there was a different (or better) option. Another adventure was in the area of Multilevel Marketing (MLM) with a company called Youngevity. Pushing health products I felt was a great spin off from pharmacy, especially the Anti-Aging concept featuring Chelated Minerals. It wasn't, however, simply about selling products, but more about building a business and leading a team. It was during this time that I felt the need to develop some speaking skills which led me to Trinity Toastmasters Club, another amazing adventure. Youngevity was a great experience, as I achieved the Two Star Gold level. My upline, Mae, told me that I was the only Black associate to do so at that time. Finally, an adventure that I had the pleasure of experiencing was to join as a background singer with the Larry 'T-Byrd' Gordon Band. Late nights in the studio while sleeping during the days was the routine. Occasionally, the lead singer pulled a 'no-show' which gave me an opportunity to lead a song or two. During my time with Birdman, I took singing lessons and keyboard lessons while the choreography was picked up on the fly. I never cashed my first paycheck so as to have proof that I was in a band. By the way, I would occasionally come across an uncashed check while going through my pile of papers. After speaking to the American Lung Association, I never got around to cashing their check. Thus, onward to the next adventure. The band played in Tyler, Houston, and of course, the Dallas Metroplex. I really enjoyed gigs in the West End of the Downtown area, in a club called Mr. 'Cs.' It was there that band leader met a rich guy from Europe who offered to fly the band there to perform. One month prior to this, I was pressured to leave the band and spend more time home with family. No regrets, as I totally enjoyed all of my adventures. As my toastmasters experience developed, I shared more of myself with my club. Although I had given my first speech (Ice Breaker) many years before, I decided to do another as I felt that I wasn't that same person. Please enjoy as I share this second Ice Breaker.

ICEBREAKER

Good Evening, Fellow Toastmasters,
The very first speech one gives after joining Toastmasters is basically to introduce him/ herself to the club. It starts the process of letting the club get acquainted with the new member. This should be the easiest speech as the new member is simply speaking about themselves or their lives. This speech we simply call the Icebreaker. Here I hope to share personal things in my life which gives insight to my unique personality as it relates to addictions. Addiction is defined as a persistent, compulsive dependence on a behavior or substance. Although there are many categories: alcohol, drugs, and others are the segments that I will use to introduce more about me as a person.

This past weekend, my entire family converged on my house for Thanksgiving. We invited a priest named Ike, who prefers Dada, which means brother. His specialty is yoga, meditation, and addictions. He gets to the house late after an alcohol addiction class. We never got to meditation which is what I thought my family would like to hear. He begins about his day and then the questions started and from there the time just seem to fly. "We give the tools to change their behavior but many relapse because the environment or simply they weren't ready to change," he states. My encounter with alcohol came when my family split. I was in and out of court, trying to get custody of my daughter. I remember drinking so much that I sought help from a friend who was an admitted alcoholic. We attended one or two AA (Alcoholics Anonymous) meetings. There I noticed that a few members were watching the clock, while fidgeting; anxious to get out and get to that drink! Pretty quickly, I knew that I was NOT an alcoholic.

I invited another man who's a successful businessman. He was a chef who catered and more recently opened his own restaurant. His amazing story begins by telling me that he was a "crackhead" for twenty-three years. "It's all I could think about. I would lie and steal, I didn't care. I even stole from my mother!" He said that he was lower than a snake's belly in a wagon rut. In his search for a solution, he found God, who gave him an outlet, the gym. He's quick to say that prayer and working out saved his life. After knowing and meeting people with this addiction, I knew that I couldn't and was too scared to try. Especially after seeing my best friend from high school get many years for a small amount of weed. I did, however, experience getting locked in jail. Into a ten-men cell, there were twenty of us. I had such a case of claustrophobia that I laid on the concrete and covered my head with my T-shirt. I nearly died of fear and knew in my heart that I couldn't be imprisoned again, so I stayed away from dope.

As I speak to people, I find that there are many other addictions: Food addictions (McDonalds/Fast Foods) which has led us to an 'obese' America. Companionship addictions are having an overwhelming need to be with someone, in a relationship. Quick note, I had a friend who said that she felt whole when she was in a relationship. That was odd for me, seeing that each of the last two relationships she had was physically violent. Either of the above could be mine, but my own personal addiction was that of pornography. I could never get enough; it was all I could think about. I sought help after what I call my darkest moment. I was sitting in church, fidgeting like the guy at the AA meeting. I could not wait to get out and get to my dirty little secret. It took a lot of soul searching, prayer, and reaching out to friends to talk. Somehow, thank God, I lost that urge! Any of us can be susceptible to any addiction. Susceptibility does not mean inevitability. Scientist are looking for the 'Addiction Gene.' If found, it would suggest that biological differences makes some folk more or less vulnerable to addiction. Remember that the environment makes up a large part of addiction risk. So, with food addictions, companionship addictions, drug/alcohol, or whatever, although we seem so different, yet we are so similar, because like me (as these experiences have shaped my personality), we all have the potential to be addicted to something.

CHAPTER 13

As we entered the new millennium, there were many concerns/fears. The thought of computer networks failing was frightening. The power systems of water, phones, railroads, airlines, trucks, stock markets, and payrolls could somehow simply go on the blink. These ideas topped the headlines of our mainstream media. I wasn't too concerned personally because of a statement in the back of my mind by Reverend Thomas Jackson of the Mt. Zion Missionary Baptist Church, which stated, "HE will take care of you...." With that, I did not stock up on food or other essentials. I do, however, view situations from a historic perspective, as many times, history repeats itself. For example, in the 1860's a surge toward civil correction culminated in the Civil War. In the 1960's a surge toward improving civil conditions culminated in the Civil Rights Movement. I did take a moment to ponder what may happen as the new millennium approaches the twenties. It was the late 1920's (1929-1941) that we dealt with a severe worldwide economic crisis that we would later call the Great Depression. As history continues to write itself, we can only wait to see. This decade began with major changes in our family. Just two years prior, (February 23, 1998) we lost our mother, Lois Doretha Yancy Porter. On October 17, 2000, we lost our daddy, Floyd Porter. On October 20, 2003, we lost our baby sister, Kathy June Porter. It was Daddy who could see distention among other families once the parents were gone. Unsure if it were from deep-seated sibling rivalry, greed, or some outside influences, but the family structure or adhesiveness seemed to fall apart. On his death bed, he requested that

61

we always stick together, because even with all our differences, he knew that we were all that we had. Often times, I had to refer back to that memory and focus on what was needed to move forward. What my father saw was a real threat. As time passed, we would test this again and again. Each time we had to come together and figure out the best way to protect our family. It began as soon as my father died; there was an immediate issue of how to distribute his property and insurance moneys. Because we had different fathers, there was a question as to who should get a portion. Once coming together, someone said simply, "remember what Daddy said!" By the way, it wasn't a heck of a lot money to begin with. Another incident related to our brother, Floyd, who had gone to prison (over and over and over again). My loving sisters would say, almost in unisons like a well-crafted song, "we just need to pray for him." They frowned as I asked, "Why? Should we continue to beg God for help? Do you think that He's not listening? Maybe that is the best place for him to detox and take time to think about his life!" I played the bad guy, suggesting that maybe God IS listening and our solution does not parallel. There was a huge argument in front of many of the kids. It had to do with whether or not to send money to support our brother in prison. One view was, "he's our brother and we must," while another was, "we've done so much and nothing has changed, so no more money from me!" As for me, a taxpayer, I felt that he was getting meals and healthcare, so to send or not to send money wasn't a major issue. It took some time, but we again came together for the good of our family. Finally, there was an issue with the homestead land. My mother's father, Wesley Yancy had acquired ninety-nine acres of land but gave his brother half. This remaining estate property with no deed is subject to auction if ever taxes aren't paid. There was a family meeting with most of the cousins, and shortly after I was asked to buy the interest of each heir with the hope of someday getting a clear deed. At that point, the land could be surveyed and divided among the heirs. I was in favor of helping with whatever, to avoid possibly losing the land later. Then came the questions: "Why does he want it?", or "Does he know how much it's worth?", and "Is he trying to get rich off of us?" This created such strife between my cousins and my siblings and myself that I backed out, facing such vitriol. In trying to understand all the pushback, I recalled a class that I had that dealt with Acquired Immune Deficiency Syndrome (AIDS). By the way, it was one of the most difficult courses that I'd ever taken.

Very broadly, I had to understand how a little virus could get into the body, attach to a protein inside the cell, make changes, then go on to affect many cells, leading to the death of the body. As such, when the individual mind of a single family member gets infected with envy, jealousy, selfishness, and yes, hatred, it can grossly change them. Everyone around them could be influenced negatively, leading to the destruction of the family unit. I'm resolved to believe that in an extreme situation or crisis, we must be of like minds, on whatever the course. One of my more recent speeches emphasized this thought. I called it 'VIRUS,' enjoy.

VIRUS

The total U.S. Covid-19 cases since the pandemic began are approaching eleven million, with 245,581 related deaths, the most in the world. The number of Covid-19 patients in U.S. hospitals has also risen to an all-time high in recent days.

Good evening Fellow Toastmasters,

I know, I know… if you're like me, you're tired of hearing the numbers: the politicizing, the social divides, and the comments by other countrymen. 'I used to want to be an American, but not anymore, or Americans have gone crazy and on and on.' I like you, just wish it was all over. Chris Rock on *Saturday Night Live*, said several times, "We can get through this!" Hoping sooner versus later.

When this all began, I left a message at the human resources department at the county hospital, asking how may I help, even as a volunteer. To me, that 'No Reply' was divine intervention, because at 65+, I probably needed to stay home. During these months, I've encountered different thoughts as to how should we handle or what should we be doing about this pandemic. There seems to be a political view, a Christian view, and an apathetic view (through fear, is no view at all). I noticed the first view when looking over a statement of my retirement account. The figures were off (in my opinion) so I called my financial planner. My odious approach of telling him how wrong my statement looked. We've known each other for years and as he began bumbling and stuttering to explain, I soon calmed down. We then exchanged pleasantries about family and work. I shared that I had been setting up at approved areas to do Covid-19 testing. I shared that this seemed to be a great opportunity for independent pharmacies to vaccinate, because for sure, the vaccine is coming! He paused and said, "If it comes, are you going to take it?" I said "Bud, there will probably be a long line!" He replied, "If the President says it's okay, I'm not gonna take it." "Hold'em up Swoll'em up! I call you with questions, and rely on answers based on logic and reason. You're saying that the opinion of one man who isn't a chemist, pharmacist, or doctor will persuade you to neglect your family's health needs!?" I wanted to switch my account away from the guy (and call Danny, our toastmaster financial leaven). The second view came as I listened to my Sunday school teacher. The general idea was to 'be obedient to civil authority.' His lesson came from Romans 13:1-7. More specifically, the second verse: Whosoever therefore resisteth the Power, resisteth the ordinance of God: and they that resist shall receive to themselves damnation. He slowed to define Power as our leaders: city council members, county commissioners, district attorneys, majors, governors, etc. Furthermore, we are resisting the authoritative order of God. He wants us to be law-abiding citizens. Simply put, the call for masks, social distancing, lowering crowd numbers in restaurants and other social gatherings should be followed. The mayor of Houston, Sylvester Turner, almost in tears on national television says, "People just won't comply!" As this happens throughout the United States, are we headed to our own damnation? I don't know.

And finally, there is the apathetic view. I'm not sure what this is based on. I've come across people, and some are healthcare professionals, who are not testing. The idea is that 'if there are no symptoms, there's no reason to test.' This raises some questions. Could one be positive and asymptomatic? If one is positive and recovers, can he/she be reinfected? Yes, answers both, so I asked, "Why not test?" One reply was "what if I'm positive?" Well, you quarantine to prevent the spread. I had the opportunity to swab for Covid at the entrance of an apartment complex in Desoto. Near the end of our day, there were calls to the office with complaints and questions like why were we there? I can only guess that there is an enormous fear of knowing or a fear of testing. Testing at some chain pharmacies, the swab (Q-tip) is given to the person to swab themselves, with their instructions of course. It can be done orally by swabbing the back of the throat, cheeks, roof of mouth, and underneath the tongue. For me,

I like the nasal swab. I explain that it doesn't hurt, only a little discomfort, enough to make a tear. I insert into one side, turning the swab four times and repeating in the other, counting to five or six each side. Both nostrils give me the most favorable specimen. This is easier than the flu shot.

It doesn't look like the virus is going away. Whatever view you take, political, Christian, or apathetic, the fastest road to a safe end is for each to stop and simply ask, "What is the best way to protect my family?" We might all end up doing the same thing and the numbers will began to fall.

CHAPTER 14

Who would have thought that retirement could come so quickly! When one approaches the age of seventy, there are so many memories, both bad ones and yet mostly good ones. So many people, places, and relationships. With no job to rush off to each day, I have to make a list of things to do or my day will go by, wasted. I still want to be productive, so I created a vision board with this partial list: restoring a 1992 Camaro RS, investing in stocks and cryptocurrency, modeling clothes, and reading of both fiction and nonfiction works, and of course, more bible study. In order to be productive, I pretend that I'm in school again and make my days follow a schedule. A time slot for reading, a time for fix-it projects, a time for the gym, etc. etc. etc. Doing many projects gives me topics to talk about in our toastmasters meetings, which began meeting in person again. During the meetings we lost a number of members. It will be a struggle to rebuild. It is difficult, week to week, to assign duties with so few people. I feel that my unspoken duty as a past president is to make sure the meetings are lively, interesting, and welcoming. Not only will I expend this to new prospective people, but to reach back in the dusty membership logs to rekindle relationships gone by. Hopefully we can find some former toastmasters, but even as I sit here, at least two phone calls inform me of persons that has passed on in my hometown.. This occurrence is more and more frequent. When I reflect on this, it brings me sadness because there were many that I knew, but not really because I only knew their nicknames. Some of the old patriarchs in my hometown had names like Scrap, Buddah, Frown, and numerous other entertaining figures of that time. Once, I received a call of the passing of a young man who attended a lower class (freshman or sophomore) during my high school years. He was younger, which surprised me. We called him Spook. It wasn't until after his death that I was told his name, John Henry. Today it is a big deal to me, as I meet and talk to people, I ask for their name. I may not remember it, but at least I heard it once. Throughout the many places one may travel, it is my desire that before reaching the age of sixty-eight, most would begin to appreciate relationships with people. It was Dr. George Fraser who suggested that we should reach out to five people from your past, each day. This strengthens ties, makes people feel good, and ultimately, we'll feel uplifted as well. Now, as for our toastmasters club, which meets again in person, my first speech was given to a skimpy group. I attempted to make it educational but mostly entertaining. It deals with relationships of sort, entitled 'Boys and Girls.'

BOYS AND GIRLS

Pleased, not only to be back, but pleased with recent speeches heard here by Cynthia, Mary, Theresa, and Jon. (Holding up three fingers on one hand and one finger on the other) Cynthia, Mary, Theresa, and Jon. Now this observation does not suggest that more good speeches will be done by the girls versus the boys in this club, although what a challenge that would be (pause and smile). Tonight, I want to explore or compare the numbers of girls versus boys around the globe, discuss how they are faring together, and finally, look at an interesting phenomenon that is occurring with boys and girls.

Good Evening Fellow Toastmasters,

I was intrigued by a recent speech on the worlds' population and how many countries lack the growth to sustain. I wanted to know more which led me to some interesting reading. In China and India, men outnumber women by seventy million. Only recently did these nations attempt to correct the policies that limited family sizes and caused this male-heavy generation. Some of the consequences, in China for example, are: the imbalance distorts labor markets, a surge in violent crimes in some areas, increase in prostitution and human trafficking, and something that is vaguely whispered, an epidemic of loneliness. A story told to me was this, Chinese men are migrating to Africa with hopes of finding female companionship. We'll have to wait to see how that turns out (pause). Along with policies to decrease birth rates, and a culture that honors the birth of boys over girls, there's the biological influence, where the sperm with the Y-chromosome moves much faster than the ones carrying the X-chromosome. Therefore, copulation several days prior to ovulation gives a higher probability of creating a girl. This is NOT NECESSARILY PRAC-TICED! All has led to this huge imbalance of the sexes.

Well, how are we faring in the unique situation? How are we getting alone? With these dynamics, you would think that women and girls should be honored, treated like queens and princesses, and also have the option to have as many mates as they want without any shame or reprimand! But NO, we are all too familiar with the plight of women in America, and more horrific situations in other countries. The Suffrage movement was a long, hard fight to seek something close to equality. Still today there are numerous organizations that promote the advancement of women, for example: Women for Women International, School Girls Unite, Every Mother Counts, and Global Fund for Women, to name a few. Divorce rates are declining as of recent years, but still there is a divorce every thirteen seconds in the USA, or 276 per hour, or 6,646 divorces per day. Looking at it another way, while standing in front of a priest or pastor, it takes two minutes on average to recite wedding vows. In that time, nine divorces have occurred. Could pastors/priests have intervened somehow to avert this end? My own naïve take on this issue is that it's all in the music. Back in my youth, the singer Al Greene sang 'I'm Tired of Being Alone' and 'Let's Stay Together.' Anita Baker sang 'You Bring Me Joy.' And we can't forget Barry White who sang, 'Darling I, Can't Get Enough of Your Love.' My oh my, someone recently said, "There just ain't no more baby making music anymore!" Today it's about violence, profanity, and some nudity. Some nudity until I saw a video of about six boys in prison dancing, without a stitch, totally nude. In one of the artists' songs, he says, "Can't nobody tell me nothing."

Recently, the mayor and the police chief of Dallas, Texas began putting together a task force that will decrease domestic abuse, which is only 25% on the list of reasons for divorce. FYI, #1 is lack of commitment (75%), and #3 is infidelity (55%). To me the numbers say, "beat on me, you can stick around, cheat on me, then I'm leaving town" Clearly boys and girls are not faring well together. Finally, I see an interesting phenomenon, where boys are falling behind! According to the National Student Clearinghouse Research Center, as of spring 2021, there is a growing gender gap in higher education. Women now account for 59.9% of students attending colleges and universities. In 1970, men at 58%, there was no great outcry. The reason for concern is in the term 'Educational Assortative Mating.' It is explained like this, if a woman has earned a four-year degree and then looks for a husband, she will usually choose a man with equal or greater educational achievement as her own. Back then, a man was happy to marry a woman who never went to college. Ever since the 1980's, boys' academic achievements in high school have slowed relative to girls. Quick note: Not primarily because girls are doing better, but because boys are doing worse. What can be done? First, schools can share some of the blame, since American schools have become unfriendly to boys. Giving reprimands for doing things that boys do, like chewing gum or doodling a picture of a gun. Parents should look for a school with a 50-50 boy-girl split in students with academic honors. Secondly, parents need to find positive role models. This may be a teacher, coach, pastor, or family friend; if lucky, the boy's father can be. Finally, moms must immerse their sons in the stories of good men. These could be from books or stories of known persons. The things I have presented suggests a bleak future at best for our boys and girls. It appears that we have been duped by politicians, pastors, and parents, with little hope for our kids and grandkids. Boys and girls, what is the real answer? What is the real answer, Boys and Girls?

Made in the USA
Middletown, DE
28 April 2023

29339302R00047